Baking Pan Dimensions	Volume	Alternative Pans
8-by-2-inch round cake pan	7 cups	14 muffins/cupcakes 28 mini muffins
9-by-2-inch round cake pan	9½ cups	8½-inch Bundt pan 8-by-8-inch baking pan
9-inch springform	10 cups	9-by-2-inch round cake pan
12-well standard muffin pan	6 cups (½ cup per well)	8-by-2-inch round cake pan 8½-by-4½-by-2½-inch loaf pan
24-well mini muffin pan	6 cups (¼ cup per well)	8-by-2-inch round cake pan 8½-by-4½-by-2½-inch loaf pan
9-by-13-inch baking pan	17¾ cups	Two 9-by-2-inch round cake pans Two 8½-inch Bundt pans Two 8-by-8-inch baking pans 36 muffins/cupcakes
8-by-8-inch baking pan	9¼ cups	9-by-2-inch round cake pan
9-by-9-inch baking pan	11¾ cups	9-inch springform 24 muffins/cupcakes
8½-inch Bundt pan	9¾ cups	8-by-8-inch baking pan 9-by-2-inch round cake pan
10-inch Bundt pan	12 cups	24 muffins/cupcakes
8½-by-4½-by-2½-inch loaf pan	6½ cups	8-by-2-inch round cake pan 11 muffins/cupcakes 22 mini muffins
9-inch standard pie pan	4½ cups	-
9½-by-1⅝-inch deep-dish pie pan	6¾ cups	-

A GOOD MEAL IS HARD TO FIND

JOURNAL

A Pocketbook of Notions & Notes

Amy C. Evans & Martha Hall Foose

CHRONICLE BOOKS

SAN FRANCISCO

CAFÉ
BUSTELO

SIEMPRE FRESCO

PESO NETO 10 OZ. (283g)

Introduction

WELCOME TO OUR POCKETBOOK OF POSSIBILITIES!

We're both list makers and doodlers, readers and road trippers, Southerners and eaters, so we wanted to create a little something special to go with our art-filled cookbook, *A Good Meal Is Hard to Find: Storied Recipes from the Deep South*. Toss this pocketbook into your purse, keep it by your bedside, or prop it up in the kitchen—put it where you will use it the most. Then, refer to it often and, most of all, fill it with words and doodles and ideas of your own.

Hopefully, once all of the pages are filled, your personal pocketbook will become a treasured keepsake—something to hold on to or hand down.

Off you go, now!

YOUR FRIENDS,

Amy & Martha

PS: Do keep in touch! You can find us at:
AGOODMEALISHARDTOFIND.COM

Birthdays

January
BIRTHDAYS

⟶≫ THE CARNATION ≪⟵

1	....	17	....
2	....	18	....
3	....	19	....
4	....	20	....
5	....	21	....
6	....	22	....
7	....	23	....
8	....	24	....
9	....	25	....
10	....	26	....
11	....	27	....
12	....	28	....
13	....	29	....
14	....	30	....
15	....	31	....
16	....		

February
BIRTHDAYS

→→ THE VIOLET ←←

1	....	17	....
2	....	18	....
3	....	19	....
4	....	20	....
5	....	21	....
6	....	22	....
7	....	23	....
8	....	24	....
9	....	25	....
10	....	26	....
11	....	27	....
12	....	28	....
13	....	29	....
14	....		
15	....		
16	....		

March

BIRTHDAYS

⇀≫ THE DAFFODIL ≪↼

1	17 ....
2	18 ....
3	19 ....
4	20 ....
5	21 ....
6	22 ....
7	23 ....
8	24 ....
9	25 ....
10	26 ....
11	27 ....
12	28 ....
13	29 ....
14	30 ....
15	31 ....
16	

April
BIRTHDAYS

→→ THE DAISY ←←

1	17
2	18
3	19
4	20
5	21
6	22
7	23
8	24
9	25
10	26
11	27
12	28
13	29
14	30
15	
16	

May

BIRTHDAYS

⟶ THE LILY OF THE VALLEY ⟵

1	17 ....
2	18 ....
3	19 ....
4	20 ....
5	21 ....
6	22 ....
7	23 ....
8	24 ....
9	25 ....
10	26 ....
11	27 ....
12	28 ....
13	29 ....
14	30 ....
15	31 ....
16	

June
BIRTHDAYS

→→ THE ROSE ←←

1		17	
2		18	
3		19	
4		20	
5		21	
6		22	
7		23	
8		24	
9		25	
10		26	
11		27	
12		28	
13		29	
14		30	
15			
16			

July
BIRTHDAYS

→→ THE LARKSPUR ←←

1	17
2	18
3	19
4	20
5	21
6	22
7	23
8	24
9	25
10	26
11	27
12	28
13	29
14	30
15	31
16	

August
BIRTHDAYS

→» THE GLADIOLUS «←

1 ....
2 ....
3 ....
4 ....
5 ....
6 ....
7 ....
8 ....
9 ....
10 ....
11 ....
12 ....
13 ....
14 ....
15 ....
16 ....

17 ....
18 ....
19 ....
20 ....
21 ....
22 ....
23 ....
24 ....
25 ....
26 ....
27 ....
28 ....
29 ....
30 ....
31 ....

September

BIRTHDAYS

⇢ THE ASTER ⇠

1	....	17	....
2	....	18	....
3	....	19	....
4	....	20	....
5	....	21	....
6	....	22	....
7	....	23	....
8	....	24	....
9	....	25	....
10	....	26	....
11	....	27	....
12	....	28	....
13	....	29	....
14	....	30	....
15	....		
16	....		

October

BIRTHDAYS

→ THE MARIGOLD ←

1	17
2	18
3	19
4	20
5	21
6	22
7	23
8	24
9	25
10	26
11	27
12	28
13	29
14	30
15	31
16	

November

BIRTHDAYS

→→ THE CHRYSANTHEMUM ←←

1	17
2	18
3	19
4	20
5	21
6	22
7	23
8	24
9	25
10	26
11	27
12	28
13	29
14	30
15	
16	

December

BIRTHDAYS

⟶⟶ THE NARCISSUS ⟵⟵

1	....	17	....
2	....	18	....
3	....	19	....
4	....	20	....
5	....	21	....
6	....	22	....
7	....	23	....
8	....	24	....
9	....	25	....
10	....	26	....
11	....	27	....
12	....	28	....
13	....	29	....
14	....	30	....
15	....	31	....
16	....		

PIMENTON
PICANTE

Mari-Paz

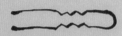

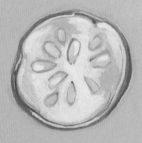

Dates

→→ TO ←←

REMEMBER

January

1

NATIONAL BLOODY MARY DAY

Make *Ferdinand's* Neat Bull Shot
from our cookbook.

27

NATIONAL CHOCOLATE CAKE DAY

Make *Flannery's* Gracious Coffee Fudge Cake
from our cookbook.

DATE   **TO REMEMBER**

February

22

NATIONAL MARGARITA DAY

Make *Rita's* Roadside Attraction
from our cookbook.

24

NATIONAL TORTILLA CHIP DAY

Make *Clementine's* H-Town Queso
from our cookbook.

DATE   **TO REMEMBER**

March

14
NATIONAL POTATO CHIP DAY
Make *Ben's* Sausage and Potato Chip Po'boy
from our cookbook.

24
NATIONAL COCKTAIL DAY
Make *Maxine's* Pin Curl
from our cookbook.

DATE

TO REMEMBER

April

3
NATIONAL CHOCOLATE MOUSSE DAY
Make *Etta's* Third-Date Chocolate Brandy Pudding
from our cookbook instead of whipping all those egg whites.

23
NATIONAL PICNIC DAY
Make *Ida's* Shore Lunch Loaf
from our cookbook.

DATE   **TO REMEMBER**

May

11

EAT WHAT YOU WANT DAY

Make *Esther's* Diminutive Crisp Corn and Curry Comeback
from our cookbook.

14

NATIONAL BUTTERMILK BISCUIT DAY

Make *Carrye's* Sugar Lump Biscuits
from our cookbook.

DATE

TO REMEMBER

June

3

NATIONAL EGG DAY

Make *Ouida's* Buttered Pimento Soufflé
from our cookbook.

1st Friday

NATIONAL DOUGHNUT DAY

Make *Francine's* Strawberry-Glazed Doughnuts
from our cookbook.

July

17

NATIONAL HOT DOG DAY

Make *Pauline's* Lucky Pickle Relish Dogs
from our cookbook.

3rd Sunday

NATIONAL ICE CREAM DAY

Make *Velma's* Secret Ice Cream Sundae
from our cookbook.

DATE   **TO REMEMBER**

August

5
NATIONAL OYSTER DAY
Make *Ula Mae's* Spoonbread with Oysters
and Artichokes from our cookbook.

24
NATIONAL WAFFLE DAY
Make *Arturo's* Buttermilk Poppy Seed Waffles
with Plum Jelly Butter from our cookbook.

DATE   TO REMEMBER

September

26

NATIONAL KEY LIME PIE DAY

Make *Ruth's* Key Lime Frappé
from our cookbook.

29

NATIONAL COFFEE DAY

Make *Loretta's* Café con Mitad y Mitad
from our cookbook.

DATE

TO REMEMBER

October

1

WORLD VEGETARIAN DAY

Make *Georgia Kay's* Marinated Green Bean Millefiori
from our cookbook.

14

NATIONAL DESSERT DAY

Make *Estelle's* Butterscotch Pound Cake
from our cookbook.

DATE

TO REMEMBER

November

3
NATIONAL SANDWICH DAY
Make *Camille's* Bridge Club Egg Salad
from our cookbook.

26
NATIONAL CAKE DAY
Make *Francesca's* Milk and Honey Cake
from our cookbook.

DATE   **TO REMEMBER**

December

30

NATIONAL BACON DAY

Make *Dot's* Sweet Potato and Bacon Purse Pie
from our cookbook.

31

NATIONAL CHAMPAGNE DAY

Make *Clara's* Oyster Shot
from our cookbook.

DATE   **TO REMEMBER**

Gift
→→IDEAS←←

GIFT IDEA #1

·· YOU'RE AN ··

Angel

AN ANTIQUE STERLING SILVER CAKE KNIFE, along with a copy of our recipe for Elise's Angel Food Cake with Raspberry Curd and a baked angel food cake, makes for a lovely hostess gift. (Use our recipe in *A Good Meal Is Hard to Find: Storied Recipes from the Deep South.*)

GIFT IDEA #2

·· **PARTY** ··

Favors

PACKAGE UP OUR JOHNNY'S SKATING RINK MINTS in pretty little bags by the handful and send them home with guests of any sort: dinner, shower, birthday, or drop-in. (Use our recipe in *A Good Meal Is Hard to Find: Storied Recipes from the Deep South*.)

GIFT IDEAS

GIFT IDEA #3

•• FIRECRACKER ••

Popcorn

FIREWORKS SHOULDN'T JUST BE FOR THE FOURTH OF JULY or New Year's Eve. Enliven any gathering with a box of Agnes's Graton Firecracker Popcorn (from *A Good Meal Is Hard to Fine: Storied Recipes from the Deep South*) and a pack of sparklers on the side.

GIFT IDEAS

·· IVY'S ··

Sweet Sausage Balls

OUR SAUSAGE BALLS are a nice addition to a brunch buffet or great as a hostess gift. (Use our recipe in *A Good Meal Is Hard to Find: Storied Recipes from the Deep South.*)

9

Party

→ PLANNING ←

Event

THEME ....

DATE ....

TIME ....

LOCATION ....

....

GUESTS ....

....

....

....

....

....

....

....

....

....

....

....

....

....

....

....

....

....

FANCY
Floaters

~~~~~~~~~~~~~~~~~~~~~~

SILICONE BAKING MOLDS of
all types are great for making
decorative ice for punch bowls.
Alternatively, you can make
ice cups in a muffin tin to float
around in your punch.

Event

THEME ....

DATE ....

TIME ....

LOCATION ....

....

GUESTS ....

....

....

....

....

....

....

....

....

....

....

....

....

....

....

IF YOU REALLY WANT
To Show Off

SERVE CORDELIA'S CORNISH HENS as an entrée with steamed asparagus and Ula Mae's spoonbread, and make Flannery's Gracious Coffee Fudge Cake for dessert (all recipes in *A Good Meal Is Hard to Find: Storied Recipes from the Deep South*).

Event

THEME ....

DATE ....

TIME ....

LOCATION ....

....

GUESTS ....

....

....

....

....

....

....

....

....

....

....

....

....

....

....

....

....

....

JUST A *Dollop*

TO DRESS UP DAINTY egg salad finger sandwiches on party rye, put a tiny dot of mayonnaise on the top of each sandwich and press a little celery or parsley leaf into each dollop.

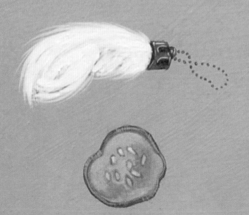

HONEYSUCKLE
Vodka

STEEP ½ CUP OF FRESH honeysuckle blossoms with the green leaves removed in 2 cups of unflavored vodka and 1 Tbsp of sugar for 24 hours. Strain and store in a capped bottle or jar in the refrigerator for a few days.

Event

THEME ....

DATE ....

TIME ....

LOCATION ....

....

GUESTS ....

....

....

....

....

....

....

....

....

....

....

....

....

....

....

....

....

DIMINUTIVE
Pot Pies

~~~~~~~~~~~~~~~~~~~~~~~~~~~~~

YOU CAN MAKE LITTLE pot pies filled with just about anything with our quickie crust (see the Reliable Recipes section). Try it with ham, cream of mushroom soup, peas, sautéed mushrooms, and green onions. Or make Vi's Sherry Pot Pie recipe (in *A Good Meal Is Hard to Find: Storied Recipes from the Deep South*).

Event

THEME ....

DATE ....

TIME ....

LOCATION ....

....

GUESTS ....

....

....

....

....

....

....

....

....

....

....

....

....

....

....

....

....

SOPHISTICATED

Spreads

IF YOU ARE FEELING extra fancy, spray a
2-cup mold or bowl with cooking oil. Line
the mold with food wrap. Place capers
or other pickled vegetables in a mosaic
pattern in the bottom of the mold. Fill it
with Joseph's Salmon Spread (in *A Good
Meal Is Hard to Find: Storied Recipes from
the Deep South*) and chill for 1 hour. Invert
the mold onto a serving plate and remove
the food wrap.

Event

THEME ....

DATE ....

TIME ....

LOCATION ....

....

GUESTS ....

....

....

....

....

....

....

....

....

....

....

....

....

....

....

....

....

A SUGARED

Rim

~~~~~~~~~~~~~~~~~~~~~~

MUSCOVADO SUGAR IS a soft, moist, dark cane sugar that tastes strongly of molasses and is produced in the Philippines and Mauritius. Aside from retaining the flavor of the cane juice, the sugar also keeps its mineral content of phosphorus, calcium, magnesium, potassium, and iron. We like to add it to our morning coffee or the rim of a cocktail glass. Muscovado sugar is widely available online and in specialty baking shops. Try it in Dolores's Vibrancy Water (in A *Good Meal Is Hard to Find: Storied Recipes from the Deep South*).

SWEET POTATO 99¢

MADE LOCALLY FRESH

SAVORY SIMON

Hubig's

New Orleans Style Pies

NET WT 4 OZ.

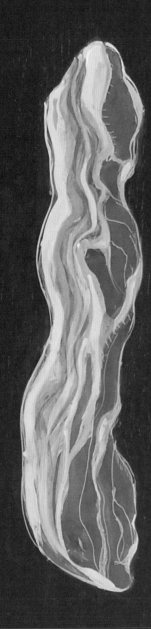

RELIABLE

Recipes

Recipe

PERFECT FOR .... PREP TIME .... COOK TIME ....

INGREDIENTS _____

METHOD _____

Carefree
COLESLAW

3 tablespoons mayonnaise

1 tablespoon rice vinegar

1 tablespoon buttermilk

1 teaspoon light brown sugar

1 teaspoon celery seeds

1 teaspoon salt

1 teaspoon dried dill

¼ teaspoon ground black pepper

⅛ teaspoon ground cayenne pepper

One 16-ounce bag tricolor coleslaw

IN A SMALL BOWL, combine the mayonnaise, rice vinegar, buttermilk, brown sugar, celery seeds, salt, dill, black pepper, and cayenne pepper. Stir to combine, then pour over the coleslaw and blend together.

NOTES

....

....

....

....

....

Easy
STRAWBERRY JAM

2 pints chopped hulled berries	Grating of nutmeg
½ cup sugar	Bit of fresh lemon juice

WHEN STRAWBERRIES ARE COMING in, make a quick jam by cooking down the berries with sugar, nutmeg, and lemon juice. You will end up with about 1¾ cups of deliciousness. Let it cool completely, then store it in the refrigerator for a week or so.

NOTES

....

....

....

....

....

....

Recipe

PERFECT FOR .... PREP TIME .... COOK TIME

INGREDIENTS _____

METHOD _____

Recipe

PERFECT FOR .... PREP TIME .... COOK TIME

INGREDIENTS _____

METHOD _____

Go-To
VINAIGRETTE

⅔ cup oil

⅓ cup vinegar

½ tablespoon minced shallot

1 teaspoon minced garlic

1 teaspoon Dijon mustard

Drop of honey

IN A JAR, COMBINE the oil and vinegar with the shallot, garlic, mustard, and honey. Shake vigorously before using, then shake before each use.

NOTES

....

....

....

....

....

....

....

One-Bowl

MUFFIN

1 cup sugar	2 teaspoons baking powder
1 cup yogurt	1 teaspoon baking soda
½ cup oil	Pinch of salt
1 egg	Fruit, nuts, or chocolate chips
2⅓ cup flour	

WHISK TOGETHER THE SUGAR, yogurt, oil, and egg. Add the flour, baking powder, baking soda, and salt. Stir until just evenly mixed. Fold in fruit, nuts, or chocolate chips. Bake at 350°F for 20 to 25 minutes.

NOTES

....

....

....

....

....

....

Recipe

PERFECT FOR .... PREP TIME .... COOK TIME

INGREDIENTS _____

METHOD _____

All-Purpose
PASTRY DOUGH

2 cups flour	¾ cup butter
1 teaspoon salt	¼ cup vegetable shortening
1 teaspoon sugar	¼ cup ice water

MIX TOGETHER THE FLOUR, salt, and sugar. Cut in the butter and vegetable shortening. Sprinkle in the ice water. Stir with a fork. Knead very briefly just to combine.

NOTES

....

....

....

....

....

....

....

Quick

QUICHE

1½ cups heavy cream

3 large eggs

Pinch of nutmeg

Pinch of salt

Pinch of white pepper

Partially baked pie crust
(see All-Purpose Pastry Dough)

WHISK TOGETHER THE HEAVY cream and eggs. Add the nutmeg, salt, and white pepper. Pour into the partially baked pie crust and bake at 375° for 25 to 30 minutes.

NOTES

....

....

....

....

....

....

Recipe

PERFECT FOR .... PREP TIME .... COOK TIME

INGREDIENTS _____

METHOD _____

Recipe

PERFECT FOR .... PREP TIME .... COOK TIME

INGREDIENTS _____

METHOD _____

Simple
STEAMED EGGS

Medium to large eggs   Bowl of ice water

PLACE YOUR EGGS IN a steamer basket set over boiling water. Cover and cook for 12 minutes. Meanwhile, fill a bowl with ice water. When the eggs are done, run them under cold water until they are cool enough to handle. Give each egg a crack and submerge them in the ice water until thoroughly chilled, 15 to 20 minutes. Peel the eggs under cold running water. For the love of all that is holy, do not overcook your eggs.

NOTES

....

....

....

....

....

....

....

BUTTER

MILK

Dictiona

Books

→ TO READ ←

Title ....

AUTHOR _____

START DATE _____ **FINISH DATE** _____ **RATING** ☆ ☆ ☆ ☆ ☆

NOTES _____

_____

_____

_____

_____

_____

_____

_____

_____

Title ....

AUTHOR _____

START DATE _____ **FINISH DATE** _____ **RATING** ☆ ☆ ☆ ☆ ☆

NOTES _____

_____

_____

_____

_____

_____

_____

_____

Title ....

AUTHOR _____

START DATE _____ **FINISH DATE** _____ **RATING** ☆ ☆ ☆ ☆ ☆

NOTES _____

_____

_____

_____

Title ....

AUTHOR _____

START DATE _____ **FINISH DATE** _____ **RATING** ☆ ☆ ☆ ☆ ☆

NOTES _____

_____

_____

_____

Title ....

AUTHOR _____

START DATE _____ **FINISH DATE** _____ **RATING** ☆ ☆ ☆ ☆ ☆

NOTES _____

_____

_____

_____

SUGGESTED READING

TITLE	AUTHOR	DATE
The Ballad of the Sad Café	Carson McCullers	1951
Bastard Out of Carolina: A Novel	Dorothy Allison	1992
Can't Quit You Baby	Ellen Douglas	1988
Cold Sassy Tree	Olive Ann Burns	1984
Delta Wedding	Eudora Welty	1946
Downhome: An Anthology of Southern Women Writers	A collection of work by 21 authors, including Eudora Welty, Bobbie Ann Mason, Zora Neale Hurston, Flannery O'Connor, and Dorothy Allison	1995
Dust Tracks on a Road: An Autobiography	Zora Neale Hurston	1942
Fair and Tender Ladies	Lee Smith	1988
A Good Man Is Hard to Find and Other Stories	Flannery O'Connor	1955
Sing, Unburied, Sing	Jesmyn Ward	2017
Southern Ladies and Gentlemen	Florence King	1975
Trials of the Earth: The True Story of a Pioneer Woman	Mary Mann Hamilton	1992

Title ....

AUTHOR _____

START DATE _____ **FINISH DATE** _____ **RATING** ☆ ☆ ☆ ☆ ☆

NOTES _____

_____

_____

_____

Title ....

AUTHOR _____

START DATE _____ **FINISH DATE** _____ **RATING** ☆ ☆ ☆ ☆ ☆

NOTES _____

_____

_____

_____

Title ....

AUTHOR _____

START DATE _____ **FINISH DATE** _____ **RATING** ☆ ☆ ☆ ☆ ☆

NOTES _____

_____

_____

_____

Title ....

AUTHOR _____

START DATE _____ **FINISH DATE** _____ **RATING** ☆ ☆ ☆ ☆ ☆

NOTES _____

_____

_____

_____

_____

_____

_____

_____

_____

Title ....

AUTHOR _____

START DATE _____ **FINISH DATE** _____ **RATING** ☆ ☆ ☆ ☆ ☆

NOTES _____

_____

_____

_____

_____

_____

_____

_____

Title ....

AUTHOR _____

START DATE _____ **FINISH DATE** _____ **RATING** ☆ ☆ ☆ ☆ ☆

NOTES _____

_____

_____

_____

Title ....

AUTHOR _____

START DATE _____ **FINISH DATE** _____ **RATING** ☆ ☆ ☆ ☆ ☆

NOTES _____

_____

_____

_____

Title ....

AUTHOR _____

START DATE _____ **FINISH DATE** _____ **RATING** ☆ ☆ ☆ ☆ ☆

NOTES _____

_____

_____

_____

Title ....

AUTHOR _____

START DATE _____ **FINISH DATE** _____ **RATING** ☆ ☆ ☆ ☆ ☆

NOTES _____

_____

_____

_____

_____

_____

_____

_____

_____

Title ....

AUTHOR _____

START DATE _____ **FINISH DATE** _____ **RATING** ☆ ☆ ☆ ☆ ☆

NOTES _____

_____

_____

_____

_____

_____

_____

_____

Title ....

AUTHOR _____

START DATE _____   **FINISH DATE** _____   **RATING** ☆ ☆ ☆ ☆ ☆

NOTES _____

_____

_____

_____

_____

Title ....

AUTHOR _____

START DATE _____   **FINISH DATE** _____   **RATING** ☆ ☆ ☆ ☆ ☆

NOTES _____

_____

_____

_____

_____

Title ....

AUTHOR _____

START DATE _____   **FINISH DATE** _____   **RATING** ☆ ☆ ☆ ☆ ☆

NOTES _____

_____

_____

_____

Title

AUTHOR

START DATE _____ **FINISH DATE** _____ **RATING** ☆ ☆ ☆ ☆ ☆

NOTES

Title

AUTHOR

START DATE _____ **FINISH DATE** _____ **RATING** ☆ ☆ ☆ ☆ ☆

NOTES

Title ....

AUTHOR _____

START DATE _____ **FINISH DATE** _____ **RATING** ☆ ☆ ☆ ☆ ☆

NOTES _____

_____

_____

_____

Title ....

AUTHOR _____

START DATE _____ **FINISH DATE** _____ **RATING** ☆ ☆ ☆ ☆ ☆

NOTES _____

_____

_____

_____

Title ....

AUTHOR _____

START DATE _____ **FINISH DATE** _____ **RATING** ☆ ☆ ☆ ☆ ☆

NOTES _____

_____

_____

_____

Title

AUTHOR

START DATE _____ **FINISH DATE** _____ **RATING** ☆ ☆ ☆ ☆ ☆

NOTES

Title

AUTHOR

START DATE _____ **FINISH DATE** _____ **RATING** ☆ ☆ ☆ ☆ ☆

NOTES

OLIVE OIL

Title ....

AUTHOR _____

START DATE _____   **FINISH DATE** _____   **RATING** ☆ ☆ ☆ ☆ ☆

NOTES _____

_____

_____

_____

_____

_____

_____

_____

_____

Title ....

AUTHOR _____

START DATE _____   **FINISH DATE** _____   **RATING** ☆ ☆ ☆ ☆ ☆

NOTES _____

_____

_____

_____

_____

_____

_____

_____

Title ....

AUTHOR _____

START DATE _____ **FINISH DATE** _____ **RATING** ☆ ☆ ☆ ☆ ☆

NOTES _____

_____

_____

_____

_____

Title ....

AUTHOR _____

START DATE _____ **FINISH DATE** _____ **RATING** ☆ ☆ ☆ ☆ ☆

NOTES _____

_____

_____

_____

_____

Title ....

AUTHOR _____

START DATE _____ **FINISH DATE** _____ **RATING** ☆ ☆ ☆ ☆ ☆

NOTES _____

_____

_____

_____

_____

BOOKS TO READ

Title ....

AUTHOR _____

START DATE _____ **FINISH DATE** _____ **RATING** ☆ ☆ ☆ ☆ ☆

NOTES _____

_____

_____

_____

_____

_____

_____

_____

Title ....

AUTHOR _____

START DATE _____ **FINISH DATE** _____ **RATING** ☆ ☆ ☆ ☆ ☆

NOTES _____

_____

_____

_____

_____

_____

_____

_____

Title ....

AUTHOR _____

START DATE _____ **FINISH DATE** _____ **RATING** ☆ ☆ ☆ ☆ ☆

NOTES _____

_____

_____

_____

_____

Title ....

AUTHOR _____

START DATE _____ **FINISH DATE** _____ **RATING** ☆ ☆ ☆ ☆ ☆

NOTES _____

_____

_____

_____

_____

Title ....

AUTHOR _____

START DATE _____ **FINISH DATE** _____ **RATING** ☆ ☆ ☆ ☆ ☆

NOTES _____

_____

_____

_____

_____

Title ....

AUTHOR _____

START DATE _____   **FINISH DATE** _____   **RATING** ☆ ☆ ☆ ☆ ☆

NOTES _____

_____

_____

_____

_____

_____

_____

_____

_____

Title ....

AUTHOR _____

START DATE _____   **FINISH DATE** _____   **RATING** ☆ ☆ ☆ ☆ ☆

NOTES _____

_____

_____

_____

_____

_____

_____

_____

_____

Title ....

AUTHOR _____

START DATE _____ **FINISH DATE** _____ **RATING** ☆ ☆ ☆ ☆ ☆

NOTES _____

_____

_____

_____

_____

Title ....

AUTHOR _____

START DATE _____ **FINISH DATE** _____ **RATING** ☆ ☆ ☆ ☆ ☆

NOTES _____

_____

_____

_____

_____

Title ....

AUTHOR _____

START DATE _____ **FINISH DATE** _____ **RATING** ☆ ☆ ☆ ☆ ☆

NOTES _____

_____

_____

_____

_____

Title ....

AUTHOR _____

START DATE _____ **FINISH DATE** _____ **RATING** ☆ ☆ ☆ ☆ ☆

NOTES _____

_____

_____

_____

_____

_____

_____

_____

_____

Title ....

AUTHOR _____

START DATE _____ **FINISH DATE** _____ **RATING** ☆ ☆ ☆ ☆ ☆

NOTES _____

_____

_____

_____

_____

_____

_____

_____

_____

Title ....

AUTHOR _____

START DATE _____ **FINISH DATE** _____ **RATING** ☆ ☆ ☆ ☆ ☆

NOTES _____

_____

_____

_____

_____

Title ....

AUTHOR _____

START DATE _____ **FINISH DATE** _____ **RATING** ☆ ☆ ☆ ☆ ☆

NOTES _____

_____

_____

_____

_____

Title ....

AUTHOR _____

START DATE _____ **FINISH DATE** _____ **RATING** ☆ ☆ ☆ ☆ ☆

NOTES _____

_____

_____

_____

Title ....

AUTHOR _____

START DATE _____ **FINISH DATE** _____ **RATING** ☆ ☆ ☆ ☆ ☆

NOTES _____

_____

_____

_____

_____

_____

_____

_____

_____

Title ....

AUTHOR _____

START DATE _____ **FINISH DATE** _____ **RATING** ☆ ☆ ☆ ☆ ☆

NOTES _____

_____

_____

_____

_____

_____

_____

_____

Title ....

AUTHOR _____

START DATE _____ **FINISH DATE** _____ **RATING** ☆ ☆ ☆ ☆ ☆

NOTES _____

_____

_____

_____

_____

Title ....

AUTHOR _____

START DATE _____ **FINISH DATE** _____ **RATING** ☆ ☆ ☆ ☆ ☆

NOTES _____

_____

_____

_____

_____

Title ....

AUTHOR _____

START DATE _____ **FINISH DATE** _____ **RATING** ☆ ☆ ☆ ☆ ☆

NOTES _____

_____

_____

_____

_____

Road

→ TRIPS ←

ROAD TRIP IDEA #1

CHASE SOME RAINBOWS

❖◆❖

EXPLORE DOLLY PARTON'S CHASING RAINBOWS MUSEUM, located at her Dollywood theme park in Pigeon Forge, Tennessee. Opened in 2002, Dolly created the museum to "share the results of her decades of dreaming, and to inspire others to follow their own." The museum includes a replica of the cabin where Dolly grew up, some of her handwritten lyrics, "Dolly's Closet," and even an interactive section where you can try on some of her wigs.

NOTES

_____

_____

_____

_____

_____

DOLLYWOOD.COM

ROAD TRIP IDEA #2

ANDALUSIA
FARM

◆◆◆

VISIT FLANNERY O'CONNOR'S HOME
in Milledgeville, Georgia. Owned by
Georgia College and State University, the
500-acre farm and 200-year-old farmhouse
are open to the public. Be sure to look for
O'Connor's typewriter and the pride of
peacocks walking the grounds. Then sit
for a spell on the lovely screened porch.

NOTES

_____

_____

_____

_____

_____

GCSU.EDU/ANDALUSIA

ROAD TRIP IDEA #3

THE
BUTTON MUSEUM

◆◆◆

SITUATED INSIDE THE VAULT of a historic bank building in St. Francisville, Louisiana, the Button Museum features thousands of antique buttons and fasteners from the 1760s through the 1940s. The collection includes rare, historic, and hand-painted buttons, as well as the owner's personal collection, which honors three generations of strong women in her family.

NOTES

_____

_____

_____

_____

_____

**GRANDMOTHERSBUTTONS.COM/
ABOUT/BUTTON-MUSEUM**

CARTER FAMILY FOLD

LOCATED IN HILTONS, VIRGINIA, the Carter Family Fold is a celebration of the Carter Family—A.P., Sara, and Maybelle Carter—America's First Family of Country Music. Every Saturday night, community members, as well as music lovers from around the world, descend on this small mountain town to listen to live music, cut a rug, and eat wonderful homemade food—hello, coconut cake!—from the concession window. The Carter Fold is family friendly, so make sure to bring the kids.

NOTES

_____

_____

_____

_____

_____

CARTERFAMILYFOLD.ORG

ROAD TRIP IDEA #5

ESSE PURSE MUSEUM

——◆◆◆——

LOCATED IN LITTLE ROCK, ARKANSAS, the Esse Purse Museum features a permanent exhibit of a century of purse styles, as well as their contents, organized by decade. Special exhibits have included themed showcases of purses in art, images and objects collected from the purses of African American women between 1891 and 1987, purses made from recycled materials, and more.

NOTES

_____

_____

_____

_____

_____

ESSEPURSEMUSEUM.COM

ROAD TRIP IDEA #6

EUDORA WELTY'S HOME & GARDEN

—◆◆◆—

LOCATED IN JACKSON, MISSISSIPPI, and designated as a National Historic Landmark, Eudora Welty's home is a real treat for fans of this beloved Southern literary icon. Welty lived here from 1925 until she passed away in 2001. Linger in the modest kitchen, peruse the thousands of books that line the walls, and then take a walk through her mother's camellia garden.

NOTES

_____

_____

_____

_____

_____

EUDORAWELTY.ORG/THE-HOUSE

ROAD TRIP IDEA #7

MAMA'S DREAM WORLD

◆◆◆

LOCATED IN BELZONI, MISSISSIPPI— also known as the Catfish Capital of the World—Mama's Dream World is home to the Ethel Wright Mohamed Stitchery Museum. The museum is the Mohamed family home and is filled with Ethel Wright Mohamed's lifework: hand-stitched narratives of family life that she lovingly called "memory pictures."

NOTES

_____

_____

_____

_____

_____

MAMASDREAMWORLD.COM

ROAD TRIP IDEA #8

MISSISSIPPI DELTA TAMALE TRAIL

— ◆◆◆ —

IF AND WHEN YOU HAVE a wild hair, take a drive through the Mississippi Delta, where you will find a particular style of tamale that took root in this part of the South more than a century ago. Make sure to visit Joe's White Front Cafe on Main Street in Rosedale, but don't forget, it's BYOT (Bring Your Own Tupperware). And definitely make our recipe for Lenore Anne's Delta Hot Tamale Balls (in *A Good Meal Is Hard to Find: Storied Recipes from the Deep South*).

NOTES

_____

_____

_____

_____

_____

SOUTHERNFOODWAYS.ORG/ ORAL-HISTORY/HOT-TAMALE-TRAIL

ROAD TRIP IDEA #9

A QUEST FOR QUESO

❖❖❖

WE CELEBRATE A PARTICULAR STYLE of
cheese dip in our book that is inspired
by the queso from the old Felix Mexican
Restaurant in Houston, Texas—a beloved
Tex-Mex spot that was opened by Felix
Tijerina in 1937 and fed Houstonians at
multiple locations for more than seven
decades. The last remaining Felix location
closed in 2008, but you can still get Felix's
World Famous Queso at El Patio, also in
Houston. See our recipe for Clementine's
Crawfish Puppies Dipped in H-Town
Queso (in *A Good Meal Is Hard to Find:
Storied Recipes from the Deep South*).

NOTES

_____

_____

_____

_____

_____

ELPATIO.COM

ROAD TRIP IDEA #10

SAVANNAH GIRL POWER

❖❖❖

FLANNERY O'CONNOR'S CHILDHOOD HOME and the home of Juliette Gordon Low, founder of the Girl Scouts, are both in Savannah, Georgia. Low, born in 1860, didn't want to use ribbons and flowers to decorate her hats, which were the fashion for ladies in her day. Instead, she decorated her hats with carrots and parsley.

NOTES

_____

_____

_____

_____

_____

JULIETTEGORDONLOWBIRTHPLACE.ORG AND FLANNERYOCONNORHOME.ORG

ROAD TRIP IDEA #11

ZORA!
FESTIVAL

◆◆◆

EATONVILLE, FLORIDA—ZORA NEALE
HURSTON'S HOMETOWN—is a tiny
community near Orlando that was the
nation's first incorporated Black township,
established in 1887. Since 1990, Eatonville
has hosted the annual ZORA! festival, a
multiday celebration of the arts, as well as
the life and work of Zora Neale Hurston.

NOTES

_____

_____

_____

_____

_____

ZORAFESTIVAL.ORG

AMY C. EVANS is an artist and a storyteller. She spent more than a decade documenting Southern food culture through oral history fieldwork, and her paintings continue to be a reflection of her explorations of the South. Amy makes her home with her daughter in Houston, Texas.

MARTHA HALL FOOSE is a cookbook author and storyteller. Her bestselling debut, *Screen Doors and Sweet Tea*, won the James Beard Award for American Cooking and the Southern Independent Booksellers Alliance Book Award. Martha makes her home with her family in the Mississippi Delta.

Chronicle Books publishes distinctive books and gifts. From award-winning children's titles, bestselling cookbooks, and eclectic pop culture to acclaimed works of art and design, stationery, and journals, we craft publishing that's instantly recognizable for its spirit and creativity. Enjoy our publishing and become part of our community at www.chroniclebooks.com.